The Ultimate Self-Teaching Metho

Play Flute

Today! Songbook

Featuring 10 Pop & Movie Favorites!

ISBN 0-634-02887-1

HAL•LEONARD®
CORPORATION
7777 W. BLUEMOUND RD. P.O. BOX 13819 MILWAUKEE, WI 53213

Visit Hal Leonard Online at
www.halleonard.com

Introduction

Welcome to the *Flute Songbook*. This book includes several well-known pop and movie favorites, and is intended for the beginner to intermediate player.

The ten songs in this book are coordinated with the skills introduced throughout levels one and two of the method, *Play Flute Today!*

Contents

About the CD

A recording of each song in the book is included on the CD, so you can hear how it sounds and play along when you're ready. Each example is preceded by one measure of "clicks" to indicate the tempo and meter. Pan right to hear the solo part emphasized. Pan left to hear the accompaniment emphasized.

4

Forrest Gump–Main Title

(Feather Theme)

from the Paramount Motion Picture FORREST GUMP

Track 1

FLUTE

Music by ALAN SILVESTRI

We Will Rock You

Track 2

FLUTE

Words and Music by BRIAN MAY

The Man From Snowy River

(Main Title Theme)

from THE MAN FROM SNOWY RIVER

Track 3

FLUTE

By BRUCE ROWLAND

My Favorite Things

from THE SOUND OF MUSIC

FLUTE

Lyrics by OSCAR HAMMERSTEIN II
Music by RICHARD RODGERS

Track 5

My Heart Will Go On
(Love Theme From 'Titanic')
from the Paramount and Twentieth Century Fox Motion Picture TITANIC

FLUTE

Music by JAMES HORNER
Lyric by WILL JENNINGS

Irish Flute/Guitar

Play

9

Colors Of The Wind

from Walt Disney's POCAHONTAS

FLUTE

Music by ALAN MENKEN
Lyrics by STEPHEN SCHWARTZ

11

Yesterday

Track 7

FLUTE

Words and Music by
JOHN LENNON and PAUL McCARTNEY

Twist And Shout

Track 8

FLUTE

Words and Music by
BERT RUSSELL and PHIL MEDLEY

Star Trek®– The Motion Picture

Theme from the Paramount Picture STAR TREK: THE MOTION PICTURE

Track 9

FLUTE

Music by JERRY GOLDSMITH

Raiders March

Track 10

from the Paramount Motion Picture
RAIDERS OF THE LOST ARK

By JOHN WILLIAMS

FLUTE

Play Flute Today!

The Ultimate Self-Teaching Method

This series provides a complete guide to the basics with quality instruction, terrific songs, and a professional-quality CD with each book. It can be used by students who want to teach themselves, or by teachers for private or group instruction. Simply follow the tips and lessons in the book as you listen to the teacher on the CD.

Level One

Your first guide to the basics includes over 70 songs and examples; how to assemble & care for the instrument; producing a sound; reading music notation and rhythms; fingering chart; glossary of musical terms.

00842043 Book/CD Pack $9.95

Level Two

Level two includes over 70 songs and examples; review of assembly & instrument care; more great music; more new notes, keys, and rhythms; fingering chart; glossary of musical terms.

00842044 Book/CD Pack $9.95

Songbook

This great supplement lets students play 10 pop and movie favorites with the accompanying CD. Songs include: Forrest Gump-Main Title • We Will Rock You • The Man From Snowy River • My Favorite Things • My Heart Will Go On • Colors Of The Wind • Yesterday • Twist And Shout • Star Trek®-The Motion Picture • Raiders March.

00842045 Book/CD Pack $12.95

FOR MORE INFORMATION, SEE YOUR LOCAL MUSIC DEALER, OR WRITE TO:

HAL•LEONARD® CORPORATION

7777 W. BLUEMOUND RD. P.O. BOX 13819 MILWAUKEE, WI 53213

Prices, contents and availability subject to change without notice. Some products may not be available outside the U.S.A.